GEORGE LUCAS

The Imagination Behind Star Wars

Rebecca Felix

Checkerboard Library

An Imprint of Abdo Publishing
abdopublishing.com

ABDOPUBLISHING.COM

Published by Abdo Publishing, a division of ABDO, PO Box 398166, Minneapolis, Minnesota 55439. Copyright © 2017 by Abdo Consulting Group, Inc. International copyrights reserved in all countries. No part of this book may be reproduced in any form without written permission from the publisher. Checkerboard Library™ is a trademark and logo of Abdo Publishing.

Printed in the United States of America, North Mankato, Minnesota

062016
092016

THIS BOOK CONTAINS
RECYCLED MATERIALS

Design: Christa Schneider, Mighty Media, Inc.
Production: Mighty Media, Inc.
Editor: Paige Polinsky
Cover Photograph: AP Images
Interior Photographs: Alamy, p. 19; AP Images, pp. 5, 13, 23, 24; Everett Collection NYC, pp. 9, 11, 19, 21; Getty Images, pp. 15, 17, 28; iStockphoto, pp. 27, 29; Yearbook Library, pp. 7, 28

Publishers Cataloging-in-Publication Data

Names: Felix, Rebecca, author.
Title: George Lucas : the imagination behind Star Wars / by Rebecca Felix.
Description: Minneapolis, MN : Abdo Publishing, [2017] | Series: Movie makers |
    Includes index.
Identifiers: LCCN 2016934270 | ISBN 9781680781854 (lib. bdg.) |
    ISBN 9781680775709 (ebook)
Subjects: LCSH: Lucas, George, 1944- --Juvenile literature. |
    Motion picture producers and directors--United States--Biography--Juvenile
    literature. | Screenwriters--United States--Biography--Juvenile literature.
Classification: DDC 791.4302/33/092 [B]--dc23
LC record available at http://lccn.loc.gov/2016934270

CONTENTS

FILM LEGEND

On a planet many **galaxies** away, a farm boy begins an adventure of a lifetime. He travels through space to save a rebel princess from an evil empire. Aliens, **androids**, and mysterious Jedi knights help him battle an evil force.

This is the world of Star Wars, one of the most successful film series of all time. George Lucas is the mind behind these space films. Lucas is a writer, **producer**, and **director**. He wrote and directed the Star Wars series. At the time, the first film, *Star Wars: Episode IV–A New Hope*, earned more money in ticket sales than any other film in history!

Lucas's work also influenced the way studios and viewers thought of movies. The technology he used inspired the future of film production. Following *A New Hope*, big-budget films began to

Director George Lucas poses with two clone troopers from his Star Wars films. Lucas's series has made more than $4 billion dollars in ticket sales.

focus more on action. Moviemakers and viewers alike were also more interested in **special effects**.

Lucas has won more than 40 film awards throughout his career. Today, he is known as a master storyteller and a leader in filmmaking. But Lucas didn't always want to make films. As a child, he had dreams of becoming a race car driver.

CALIFORNIA RACER

George Walton Lucas Jr. was born in Modesto, California, on May 14, 1944. He was the only son of George Sr. and Dorothy Lucas. George Jr. had three sisters, Wendy, Katherine, and Ann.

The Lucases owned a walnut ranch. They also owned an office supply store. They raised their children in a small farming community outside Modesto. George's family sometimes took trips into town to see movies. But they didn't own a television until George was about ten years old.

George had many different hobbies as a child. He spent much of his time reading and drawing. He even thought about becoming an illustrator

George's senior yearbook photo

one day. George also built things out of wood, such as chess sets. But most of all, George dreamed of being a race car driver.

George was devoted to cars throughout his teenage years. While attending Thomas Downey High School, he took several auto mechanics courses. He raced many of the cars he worked on. One of these, a little Italian car, was a gift from his father. But one terrible ride would steer George's interests in a new direction.

LIFE-CHANGING
CRASH

On June 12, 1962, a terrible accident happened. Lucas was just days from graduating high school. He was driving home from class in his speedy Italian car. But right before Lucas reached his driveway, another car hit his car.

Lucas was thrown from the automobile and badly injured. He was rushed to a hospital, where he remained for several weeks. He missed his final exams and graduation ceremony. However, the school still let Lucas graduate.

Experiencing such a serious accident changed Lucas's attitude. Up until then, he had been focused on having fun. After the crash, he took life more seriously. "When you go through something like that, it puts a little more **perspective** on things, like maybe you're here for a reason," he said.

Lucas later recreated his car crash for a scene in the film *American Graffiti* (*above*). In both crashes, the car flipped over many times.

Lucas discovered his reason as he spent the summer recovering. During this time, he watched a lot of television and movies. He became **passionate** about films. Lucas decided to let go of his race car dreams and become a filmmaker.

In the fall of 1962, Lucas began attending Modesto Junior College. He was an art major. Two years later, he transferred to San Francisco State University. After a short time there, he switched to the University of Southern California (USC) in Los Angeles.

Lucas studied **cinematography** at USC. While there, he made several successful short movies. In 1965, Lucas wrote and **directed** a short called "Look at Life." The film was very popular with his professors and classmates. He also wrote and directed a 15-minute science-fiction film, "Electronic Labyrinth: THX-1138:4EB."

Lucas graduated from USC in 1966. By then, his work had caught the attention of major film executives. In 1967, film studio Warner Brothers awarded Lucas an **internship**. He would study directing on the **set** of the movie *Finian's Rainbow.*

SUPER SHORT

"Look at Life" was only one minute long. It was a fast-paced look at culture in the 1960s. The photos paired with music had a powerful effect on viewers. The film's peculiar style inspired the entire animation department at USC.

Lucas (*left*) was determined to do what he loved. But his

FIRST FILMS

Francis Ford Coppola, the **director** of *Finian's Rainbow*, became an advisor to Lucas. After the **internship**, Coppola made Lucas his assistant on another film. Lucas filmed the experience. In 1968, he released a **documentary** about Coppola called *Film Maker*.

That same year, Lucas's short film "Electronic Labyrinth: THX-1138:4EB" won the annual National Student Film Festival, held in New York City. The film interested Coppola. He and Lucas decided to start a production company together.

In 1969, Lucas and Coppola moved to Northern California. There, they opened production company American Zoetrope. The company began making a full-length version of Lucas's film, now titled *THX 1138*. Later in 1969, Lucas married film editor Marcia Griffin.

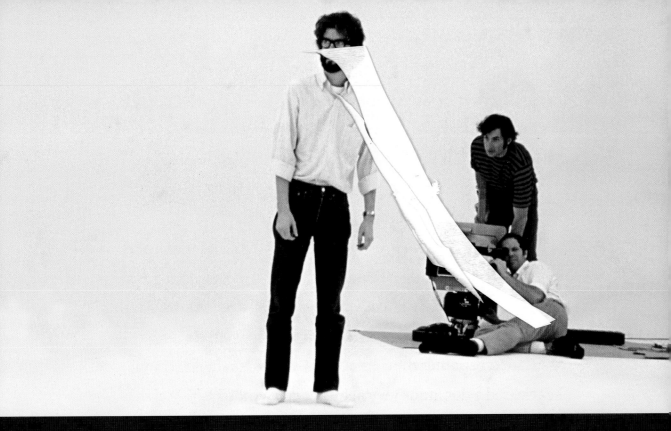

Lucas on the set of *THX 1138*. The film takes place in a harsh, controlling future society.

THX 1138 did not do well at its 1971 release. Lucas was disappointed, but he didn't give up. Instead, that year he began his own production company, Lucasfilm. The company's first film, *American Graffiti*, was inspired by Lucas's teenage **passion** for cars. The movie would be his first financial success.

Lucas wrote, **directed**, and edited *American Graffiti*. Coppola was the **producer**. The film follows a group of teenagers as they drive around their small California town. The cars and setting were similar to those from Lucas's childhood. He felt a very personal connection to the film.

At its 1973 release, *American Graffiti* was a hit. The film made millions of dollars in ticket sales. And in 1974, it was nominated for five **Academy Awards**, also known as Oscars. These included Best Picture, Best Director, and Best **Screenplay**. Lucas finally felt he had succeeded in the film industry.

American Graffiti's popularity opened doors for Lucas. He had officially proven himself as a major Hollywood director. Now he could work on any project he wanted. And his next project would become a greater success than he could have imagined.

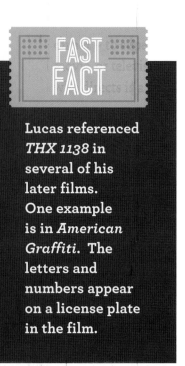

STAR WARS

Lucas's next project was unlike anything anyone had ever imagined. He began writing *Star Wars*, a **galactic** fantasy story. The story was originally planned as a children's cartoon for television. But as he was writing, Lucas changed his mind. He would turn his story into one of the most amazing adventures in film history.

Many studio executives didn't understand the project. But based on *American Graffiti*'s success, film studio 20th Century Fox agreed to fund the film. Lucas spent the next four years **directing** and **producing** *Star Wars*. In 1975, he started Industrial Light & Magic, a part of Lucasfilm, to create the **special effects**.

When *Star Wars* released in 1977, it was an instant hit. Viewers had never seen such special effects. And the effects were

Lucas and his wife, Marcia, edit *Star Wars* together. Marcia was one of the film's lead editors.

combined with an exciting, fast-paced story. Audiences were amazed by the constant sounds, effects, and action.

    Star Wars made $513 million in ticket sales. It won seven **Academy Awards**. Endless *Star Wars*-related products were made and sold. Lucas had created a film that changed the history of the movie industry.

ON THE SET OF
STAR WARS

*S*tar Wars was filmed around the world, beginning in Tunisia. The first day of **shooting** took place there on March 22, 1976. The desert represented fictional planet Tatooine in the film.

The crew's first day of filming began at 6:30 a.m. But as the day's work began, the crew ran into several problems. Some **androids'** batteries were dead and could not be replaced. Other androids would not respond to their remote controls.

As **director**, it was up to Lucas to solve any problems on **set**. He found creative ways to shoot the androids as needed for the scene. This included using ropes to pull the broken androids through the scenes. Meanwhile, Lucas oversaw the setting, actors, crew, costumes, location, story, and sound.

Lucas and actor Anthony Daniels, who plays robot C-3PO. Daniels's uncomfortable costume required many adjustments.

Lucas inspects a model of the Death Star. The Death Star is both a space station and a major weapon in the Star Wars series.

Later in the day, a desert storm tore through the **set**. The bad weather ruined some of Lucas's work. He quickly began **reshooting** or rewriting these scenes.

Despite many obstacles, Lucas continued to find ways to bring his vision to life. After more than 12 hours, the first day came to an end. And after three years of production, *Star Wars* was complete.

SERIES SUCCESS

After *Star Wars* was released, other movie studios hurried to make science-fiction films. Many wanted Industrial Light & Magic to create their films' **special effects**. Lucasfilm's technology was always ahead of the competition.

While managing Lucasfilm, Lucas wrote two more Star Wars movies. *Star Wars: **Episode** V–The Empire Strikes Back* was released in 1980. In 1981, the first Star Wars film was rereleased as *Star Wars: Episode IV–A New Hope*. That same year, Marcia and Lucas also adopted a daughter, Amanda.

Marcia and Lucas divorced in 1983. In May of that year, *Star Wars: Episode VI–The Return of the Jedi*, **premiered**. In between his work on Star Wars, Lucas began another bestselling series.

Lucas and actor Harrison Ford (*right*) on the set of *Raiders of the Lost Ark*. Ford played the title character in the Indiana Jones films. He also starred in the Star Wars series.

Lucas wrote a **screenplay** about an adventurer named Indiana Jones. Friend and fellow **director** Steven Spielberg joined Lucas to make the first film. *Raiders of the Lost Ark*, released in 1981, was a huge sensation. It became the first in a series of Indiana Jones films. The films joined Star Wars as one of the most popular series of all time.

GOLDEN YEARS

In the mid-1980s, Lucas decided to focus on his production company. So, he developed Skywalker Ranch in Nicasio, California. It served as headquarters for Skywalker Sound, Lucasfilm's sound effects and music recording division.

Lucas continued to **produce** many movies. But being a good father was his main goal. In 1988, he adopted daughter Katherine. Five years later, Lucas adopted a son, Jett.

Through the 1990s, Industrial Light & Magic created **special effects** for more than 100 films! These included 1993's *Jurassic Park* and 1995's *Jumanji*. Special effects were quickly improving, and the new technology inspired Lucas. In 1997, he added computer effects to the Star Wars **trilogy**. He then rereleased the films in theaters.

George Lucas, Carrie Fisher (*second from right*), and Mark Hamill (*right*) at the Star Wars Trilogy Special Edition world premiere in Los Angeles, California

23

Lucas receives the Galactic Achievement Award at the ShoWest Award Show in Las Vegas, Nevada.

Critics and fans did not appreciate the altered films. Many preferred the original movies they knew and loved. The advancing technology also inspired Lucas to write more Star Wars films. These films brought Lucas back to **directing** for the first time in 20 years.

Lucas wrote and directed three new Star Wars movies. They are **prequels** to the original films. In 1999, *Star Wars: **Episode** I–The Phantom Menace* was released. It was the second-highest earning movie at the time.

The prequels didn't always receive the best reviews. But all three films sold well in theaters. The final film, *Star Wars: Episode III–Revenge of the Sith*, came out in 2005. Many felt the movie did a good job of completing the series.

CRITICS REACT

"*The Phantom Menace* is probably one of the most **deliriously inventive films to have appeared in years: it displays all of George Lucas's uncommon magic, a wide-eyed genius for adventure. . . . It is daring and beautiful.**"

—Andrew O'Hagan,
The Telegraph

"**The three Star Wars prequels Lucas released . . . were among the most eagerly awaited movies of all time—and arguably, among the most disappointing movies of all time. . . . [Was] it worth all that to sully the memories of the original trilogy with a deluge of inferior sequels . . . ?**"

—Gary Susman,
Time

The writers both reviewed *The Phantom Menace,* but their opinions are very different. Consider both sides. Who makes a better argument? Do you agree with one review more than the other? Why?

LIFELONG LEGACY

Lucas wasn't done reinventing his old projects. In 2008, he returned to Indiana Jones. He **produced** *Indiana Jones and the Kingdom of the Crystal Skull*. It was the fourth film in the series.

In 2012, Lucas sold Lucasfilm to Walt Disney Company. The following year, Lucas married Mellody Hobson at Skywalker Ranch. The couple had a daughter, Everest, the same year.

The Walt Disney Company released the seventh Star Wars film, *Star Wars: The Force Awakens*, in 2015. Lucas was not involved in making the movie. At first, his reaction to *The Force Awakens* was not positive. But he later said that he was very proud of its **director**, J.J. Abrams.

FAST FACT

Lucas earned $4.05 billion from the Lucasfilm sale. He donated most of the money to charity.

Mellody Hobson and Lucas attend the 2008 Cannes International Film Festival in Paris, France.

Today's Star Wars filmmakers are continuing the Lucas **legacy**. But they have a challenge ahead of them. George Lucas's work changed the history of **cinema**. It also influenced **cultures** worldwide. People across the planet recognize Lucas and the marvels that began in his moviemaker's mind.

TIMELINE

1944

George Walton Lucas Jr. is born in Modesto, California, on May 14.

1966

Lucas graduates from the University of Southern California.

1967

Lucas begins a film internship with Warner Brothers Studios.

1969

Lucas marries Marcia Griffin.

1971

Lucas creates production company Lucasfilm.

1975

Lucas creates Industrial Light & Magic, a special effects division of Lucasfilm.

FAMOUS WORKS

American Graffiti
Released 1973

Lucas missed his high school reunion while filming.

Won: Best Motion Picture — Comedy or Musical, Golden Globes, 1974

Star Wars: Episode IV— A New Hope
Released 1977

Some theaters showed this film for more than a year.

Nominated: Best Director, Academy Awards, 1978

Raiders of the Lost Ark
Released 1981

Lucas had the idea for Indiana Jones around the same time he had the idea for Star Wars.

Nominated: Best Picture, Academy Awards, 1982

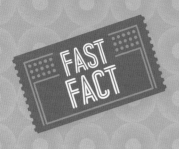

FAST FACT

Lucas founded The George Lucas Educational Foundation in 1991. It is a charity that helps students become active, engaged learners.

1977

Lucas's *Star Wars: Episode IV–A New Hope* is released.

1981

Lucas and Marcia adopt a daughter, Amanda.

1983

Star Wars: Episode VI– Return of the Jedi premieres. Lucas and Marcia divorce.

1988

Lucas adopts a daughter, Katherine.

1993

Lucas adopts a son, Jett.

2013

Lucas weds Mellody Hobson. The couple has a daughter, Everest.

Star Wars: Episode VI– Return of the Jedi
Released 1983

First film to earn more than $20 million its opening weekend.

Won: Favorite Motion Picture, People's Choice Awards, 2006

Star Wars: Episode I– The Phantom Menace
Released 1999

This film features visual effects in every scene except one.

Nominated: Best Visual Special Effects, BAFTA Awards, 2000

Star Wars: Episode III– Revenge of the Sith
Released 2005

The original version of the film ran four hours long.

Won: Favorite Motion Picture, People's Choice Awards, 2006

GLOSSARY

Academy Award – one of several awards the Academy of Motion Picture Arts and Sciences gives to the best actors and filmmakers of the year.

android – a robot that looks like a person.

animation – a process involving a projected series of drawings that appear to move due to slight changes in each drawing.

cinema – the movie industry. *Cinematography* is the art and science of photographing motion pictures.

critic – a professional who gives his or her opinion on art, literature, or performances.

culture – the customs, arts, and tools of a nation or a people at a certain time.

deliriously – marked by the inability to think straight because of either a high fever or extreme happiness.

deluge – a large amount of something.

direct – to supervise people in a play, movie, or television program. Someone who directs is a *director*.

documentary – a film that artistically presents facts, often about an event or a person.

episode – one of the programs in a television or movie series.

galaxy – a very large group of stars and planets. Something from or relating to a galaxy is *galactic*.

internship – a program in which a student or graduate gains guided practical experience in a professional field.

WEBSITES

To learn more about Movie Makers, visit booklinks.abdopublishing.com. These links are routinely monitored and updated to provide the most current information available.

legacy – something important or meaningful handed down from previous generations or from the past.

passion – great devotion or enthusiasm. Someone who has much enthusiasm is *passionate*.

perspective – a particular attitude toward or way of looking at something.

premiere – to have a first performance or exhibition.

prequel – a movie or book that tells the part of a story that happened before the story in another movie or book.

produce – to oversee staff and funding to put on a play or make a movie or TV show. Someone who produces is a *producer*.

screenplay – the written form of a story prepared for a movie.

sequel (SEE-kwuhl) – a book, movie, or other work that continues the story begun in a preceding one.

set – an artificial setting where a play is performed or a movie or television program is filmed.

shoot – to film a movie or video.

special effects – visual or sound effects used in a movie or television program.

sully – to damage or ruin the good quality of something.

trilogy – a series of three novels, movies, or other works that are closely related and involve the same characters or themes.

INDEX